Around & About
SALCOMBE

Chips Barber
and
Sally Barber

GW00726133

OBELISK PUBLICATIONS

OTHER BOOKS BY CHIPS BARBER:
Around & About Sidmouth
Around & About Seaton and Beer
Around & About Teignmouth and Shaldon
The Lost City of Exeter
Diary of a Dartmoor Walker / Diary of a Devonshire Walker
The Great Little Dartmoor Book / The Great Little Exeter Book
Made in Devon, (with David FitzGerald)
Dartmoor in Colour
Burgh Island and Bigbury Bay (with Judy Chard)
Dark & Dastardly Dartmoor (with Sally Barber)
Exeter in Colour / Torbay in Colour
The Ghosts of Exeter (with Sally Barber)
The Great Little Totnes Book (with Bill Bennett)
Tales of the Teign (with Judy Chard)
Ten Family Walks on Dartmoor (with Sally Barber)
The Great Little Plymouth Book / Plymouth in Colour
Weird & Wonderful Dartmoor (with Sally Barber)
Ghastly and Ghostly Devon (with Sally Barber)
Dawlish and Dawlish Warren
The South Hams
Torquay / Paignton / Brixham
Ten Family Walks in East Devon (with Sally Barber)
OTHER BOOKS ABOUT THIS AREA FROM OBELISK PUBLICATIONS:
Walks in the South Hams, Brian Carter
Under Sail Through South Devon & Dartmoor, Raymond B. Cattell

For further details of any of our titles, please contact us at the address below or telephone Exeter (0392) 468556

ACKNOWLEDGEMENTS
All colour photographs by Chips Barber
Sketch maps by Sally Barber
Drawing on page 22 by Andrea Barber
Thanks to Betty Smaridge and Peggy Weston for loan of old pictures

First published in 1993 by
Obelisk Publications, 2 Church Hill, Pinhoe, Exeter, Devon
Designed by Chips and Sally Barber
Typeset by Sally Barber
Printed in Great Britain by
Sprint Print Co Ltd, Okehampton Place, Exeter

Around & About Salcombe

Anyone who knows South Devon would surely list Salcombe amongst their favourite towns! It is a place of gorgeous scenery, beautiful walks and magic memories. But when it comes to writing a book about this Devonshire paradise, it is not enough to simply use guide-book phraseology on every page. That would tell us nothing of the town's past. So this book will attempt to give everyone a glimpse of what the place is really all about. I have also tried to capture the mood of Salcombe with photographs, so that all those holiday visitors who have returned home, will have something to remind them of this wonderful small port and yachting haven.

I have collected all sorts of stories for *Around and About Salcombe*. Inevitably most of them deal with Salcombe's wheelings and dealings with the sea, as it is this, above all, which reflects the very nature of the place. However, the book ends with three short walks for you to try and these, if you get a good day, are worth the purchase price of the book on their own! Well I think so anyway…

We start by going back about four hundred years to a very different Salcombe. Many people seek the peace and quiet of Salcombe as a sanctuary, a place to live that is incredibly beautiful and extremely mild. How different it must have been in 1607 when a report of the Quarter Sessions singled out the town as being, "full of dissolute sea-faring men, who murdered each other and buried them in the sands by night!"

Salcombe is the last place on earth you would imagine warring factions staging a battle, but it was! As the English Civil War (1642-1646) reached its last few months, the Parliamentary forces went round mopping up the last vestiges of resistance. Nobody considered Fort Charles as an obstacle in the triumphant march westwards of the Roundheads, and the taking of it was regarded as a formality. But this was not to be the case.

The little fort had begun the war as a ruin, but an investment of serious money had fortified it to the extent that it was not easily going to capitulate. A large sum of money had also been also spent on the fort's arsenal and provisions to see out any prolonged assault. Spoiling tactics and a determined attitude by Sir Edward Fortescue, in charge of the fort, meant the siege was a long one. The sixty-six stout Royalists were prepared to go the distance and no amount of attacks or pressure could persuade them otherwise. Sir Thomas Fairfax must have been terribly frustrated at not being able to capture this

stronghold. And they also had to contend with the two laundresses, Mary Brown and Elizabeth Terry, outnumbered by thirty-three to one in the gender stakes!

For four months the Roundheads plotted and attacked from their headquarters on Rickam Common, on the east side of the water. Despite a lot of noise and the use of a lot of ammunition, only two men were killed, one on each side. Samuel Stodard was the unlucky Royalist victim, whilst Philip Hingston was hit by a pot shot, through one of the seven loop-holes for musketry fire, as he approached the fort.

The luckiest escape was experienced by Sir Edmund, who, fed up with all the attacks, went to bed to get a bit of peace and quiet. A bullet ricocheted off a wall and blasted off one of his legs… that is one of the legs on his bed!

Eventually the two sides agreed a compromise. The Royalists negotiated favourable and honourable terms for their surrender. Ten articles or conditions were accepted and the men, with their flag held high, in good voice, were allowed to walk unharmed out of the last Royalist outpost in Devon (Pendennis in Cornwall had yet to capitulate) and up to Fallapit, the home of Sir Edmund. Here they disbanded and were free to get on with their lives.

The fort had been a real thorn in the side of the Parliamentary forces and it was no surprise when Colonel Wheldon had it dismantled. Sir Edmund wisely decided not to stay in England but went to Holland. As a souvenir, he kept the 16-inch key to the castle, which is possibly still a Fortescue family heirloom. At the time of the civil war it is likely that the population of this settlement was less than two hundred.

The town recovered from its involvement and resumed its maritime activities, slowly building up trade in both fishing and, more importantly, ship-building. One unusual industry of the town was the dredging of sand, from a point close to the dreaded bar. In 1776-77 as many as thirty-two barges collected sand which was taken to be used as fertiliser on fields in the area. This sea manure had many excellent properties, provided, of course, that you were up wind from it!

By 1791 the air had cleared and there were fifty properties in Salcombe, which housed a total of about three hundred people. The little port was growing apace until, by the turn of the century, it had reached five hundred.

However, the fighting qualities of Salcombe men were evident again when a French brig got into trouble and ran on to the sunken rock known as The Rickham. Whole streets of men armed themselves with cutlasses and went after the French vessel. In no time they had captured the ship and had taken it back to Salcombe as a trophy of war. For their gallant and brave efforts, every man was given a monetary reward.

So all seemed well with the world as Salcombe possessed the right credentials to enter the Victorian era with the right basis for a rosy future. Closeness to the sea, a sheltered location, and the availability of natural resources fuelled further impetus.

Timber was an all important commodity and the area was fortunate in being blessed with woodlands conveniently located near the many 'fingered' estuary. When better quality timber was required it was imported from Canada or taken from large oak woods in the vicinity of Kingsbridge. But it was a tough and dangerous task to transport the timber from these oak woods down to Salcombe. A report in the *Salcombe Times*, in 1837, reported that four local men drowned when their small craft, which was towing a flotilla of timber, was capsized in a blizzard, by a strong easterly wind. Their bodies were recovered from the mud at low tide. Two thousand mourners attended the joint funerals of John Harris, John Putt, Thomas Luckham and James March.

The name Sawyer, common in the area, derives from the trade of sawing the timber in specially constructed pits where pit-sawyers laboured hard and long at their trade. They cut the timber into planks, which were then placed into the 'steaming box', a device which made them pliable. Prepared to the demands of the craftsmen, the ships were built with skill and launched with pride! However not every launch went

smoothly. The *Lady Agnes* showed a certain reluctance to enter the water. The problem lay with the greasy slip that she was supposed to slide down – it simply wasn't greasy enough. You can imagine the panic that set in amongst those charged with the task of dispatching the vessel. Boys were sent to run around all the houses nearby to get whatever candles they could acquire. After a frantic few minutes the slipway was rendered sufficiently slippery for *Lady Agnes* to slide gracefully down into the water in a fashion becoming to her name.

In 1860 it was estimated that 150 vessels could be accommodated at Salcombe, in

water that ranged from a depth of four to seven fathoms. Boats up to about seventy tons could get up to Kingsbridge. Not only that, but many of the vessels going to and from the port were built there.

It is hard, these days, to imagine Salcombe as primarily a shipbuilding settlement but it was in the mid-nineteenth century when four yards competed rigorously for any available work. The speciality was the Salcombe clipper, a fast ship, if handled properly, which could reach destinations quickly and transport cargoes at a pace that endeared merchants to them. With ships being built ranging from between 100 to 550 tons there was plenty of hard work for the men of the port either on 'terra firma' or at sea. At that time Salcombe had a thousand sailors! It owned 25,000 tons of shipping and its waterfronts were the scene of intense activity.

A list of the far-away places that traded with Salcombe would include the West Indies, North and South America, many Mediterranean ports, in fact almost everywhere in the world! In addition there were ships from less exotic locations, grimy coal barges nestling up beside the Custom House Quay, having come from the Newcastle area.

What a scene it must have been on those Salcombe quays of yesteryear: silks from Taranto; ginger from Barbados; rubber from Para; oil from Cartoforte; raisins from Patras; coffee, cocoa and tobacco from Puerto Rico; molasses and rum from Antigua; arrowroot from Elenthora; lime juices and spices from Dominica; timber, fruit and cotton from the USA; meat, grain, coffee and hides from South America; oranges from The Azores; wine, velvet, oil and marble from the Mediterranean.

The ideal cargo for a fast Victorian clipper was a perishable one, they were the best ships for the job. This is an extract from a book called *Blue Water Ventures* by Captain Ryder, published in 1931, about the trading of fruit in those halcyon days of graceful, sleek sailing vessels: "*We would sail out with a cargo of coal from Cardiff to the West Indies and then load sugar, fruit and rum. In those ships also oranges would be fetched from St Michael's, Azores, and the voyage home would be kept as secret as possible. In order to get to the London market before it was known that the ship had even reached home waters, she would refrain altogether from signalling passing vessels or shore stations. If there was a risk of being reported, we would often cover our ship's name up with a board. Nevertheless the crew of any craft which passed to leeward of a fruiter laden with pineapples realised the cargo at once. As a bit of an advertisement one of these Salcombe vessels would, on coming up the Thames, display one of the biggest pineapples at the end of her jib-boom. Those were the days of real seamanship, when these handy clever little ships would despise the services of a tug, and come along through the traffic and strong tide under their own sail right up to Fresh Wharf by London Bridge.*"

Captain Ryder went on to extol the virtues of the vessels: "*With their tall masts, their shapely yards, well-kept hulls and smart canvas, these Salcombe fruiters were beautiful to behold. Spars* [the maritime, not the supermarket type!] *were kept scraped and varnished, and everything was taut and trim from truck to deck. Some of them by their very names indicated pride of origin: "Queen of the West," "Queen of the South," "Salcombe Castle"* [which met her demise on the coast of New Zealand on 15 September 1863], *"Western Belle," "Avon"* [after the river which flows into the Channel to the west of Salcombe], *"Lord Devon," "Malborough," "Erme"* [another river further west].*" And so it went on, proud vessels Salcombe-built, and as often as not Salcombe sailed!

But it was not always as romantic or as clear cut as it might sound. There were hardships, there were tough times both in the port and out on the storm-tossed seas. A number of Salcombe sailors set sail only to perish in distant parts. The Salcombe brig, the *Creole*, sank without trace on the homeward leg of a journey from the West Indies but this was accepted as an occupational hazard.

The person who named the Salcombe-registered vessel, the *Neptune*, probably thought that here he had a craft able to defy the waves. What he didn't allow for was the fact that the ship would catch on fire at Salcombe! The mate cut her moorings and she drifted ashore, burnt out and sank. What a waste of nine tons of beer!

Salcombe was all hustle and bustle. It was a busy hive of shipbuilding and the unmistakable sound of the caulking mallet, the smell of pitch and tar, or the sight of real artists at work with the adze, were normal experiences to the inhabitants.

This generated a lot of activity and it was very much the golden age of Salcombe as a port with the air filled with the smells of the many and various cargoes, and the sounds of the shore-side activities. Ship-building went on apace and in tandem with that went all the allied trades of rope and sail-making, smiths and suppliers.

But it wasn't to be a lasting prosperity...

About a century ago, *Kelly's Directory* for Devon described Salcombe as follows: *"Salcombe is a sub-port of Dartmouth and the chief port of the Kingsbridge district and has its own registration of shipping, a custom house, and coastguard station. The harbour, although capable of receiving vessels of a large tonnage, is better adapted for ships of average size, owing to the narrowness and the intricasies of navigation which are presented by large rocks which lie at the entrance. The climate of this district is very mild; the American aloe blooms in the open air and oranges, lemons and citrons reach a state of ripe perfection, and in this circumstance, combined with the beauty of the surrounding scenery, has of late brought it into favour as a watering place."*

This most southerly of Devonshire towns was remote in Victorian times, the main contact with the outside world being through the steamer, the *Kingsbridge Packet*, daily up and down the estuary to Kingsbridge or twice weekly to Plymouth, these voyages having set off from Kingsbridge Quay first.

The natural way to get to Kingsbridge in the mid-nineteenth century was by water, for it was far more direct than detouring around all the fingers of the creeks. Row boats were used at first and competition for passengers between the various ferrymen was keen. Poor Mr March usually had his share of male passengers but could not compete with Edward Woods who was so handsome that young ladies went to Kingsbridge just so they could gaze on him! However when steamers replaced the hard slog of rowing all the way, the name March, of Union Street, Salcombe was still in the business of conveying passengers to Kingsbridge but there was no mention of the dashing Edward Woods!

It was the practice in Victorian Salcombe to celebrate birthdays or glad tidings in the port by decking out all the ships and boats with bunting and other forms of decoration. Those who went by road in 1894 had first hand experience of the trials and tribulations of travelling in less than comfortable conveyances, *"... I at last decided to visit Salcombe. I went to Kingsbridge by train and proceeded thence by what, for courtesy's sake, is called a 'coach'. This consisted of a rattletrap box on wheels which would be a disgrace to any place. I am told that an improvement in this direction will be made. Squeezed, jolted and cross, I and my friend arrived at the Marine Hotel."*

Another few years passed and the *Western Morning News,* in an article published in early July 1896, included these observations, which revealed that things were stirring:

"... not so many years since Salcombe was scarcely known to the outside world. It is not by any means 'discovered' yet. There was one thing which tended to keep its existence in the memory of a few. This was shipbuilding. Yes. One would scarcely imagine such a peaceful old spot and old-world looking village had once earned itself a famous name for its wooden clippers, many of which eventually found their way to the Mediterranean. The whole settlement today suggests an out-of-the-way fishing village. Singularly enough this has never formed part of the industry of the place. Fishing there is, yet only of a desultory character. But little – scarcely anything, indeed – remains of the shipbuilding industry. The advent of steam and iron ships killed it and the prospects of Salcombe at one and the same time. Time was when the old fashioned houses of Salcombe proper, with its little narrow streets and passages, were filled with master mariners and sailors of the mercantile marine. But the collapse of shipbuilding drove them away. Salcombe, to put it popularly, appeared to be 'going to the dogs' as far as the town was concerned. Houses remained unoccupied and fell into disrepair. To stop the rot alternatives were discussed and serious thought was given to the idea of building iron ships, Snapes Point being the favoured location for such a venture. It was only when the economics of such an enterprise were given close consideration that it was realised that Salcombe would never be able to compete as the raw materials were too far away and too expensive to haul to the southernmost tip of Devon. Thus the thriving little port of Salcombe became a ghost town and the population dwindled as men left it in search of work elsewhere.

"For years the place remained 'undiscovered' and unthought of by the energetic tourist. However its potential was recognised by Dr John Huxham, an eminent Plymouth physician in the reign of George II. He saw enough similarities in both the landscape and climate to proclaim that Salcombe was 'The Montpellier of England!'

"At length the horizon cleared. The Earl of Devon's estate above the old town – stretching out to Bolt Head – one day came onto the market. A company was formed in London, and it at once purchased eighty-eight acres of land near the town. The directors of the South Devon Land Company saw their opportunity. What is perhaps better, they seized it. To employ a modern colloquialism, they began to 'boom' Salcombe. This was the only remedy for the decay and neglect of so charming a spot."

The article went on to point out that the development should continue in a cautious fashion as constructing properties that would never be occupied was a waste of time. However it was optimistic that Salcombe did have a future and added, *"Salcombe will, at no very distant date, develop into what Nature has most fitted it for. It will be a second Torquay – perhaps 'The Princess of Watering Places'* [Torquay being the Queen!] *for no-one wants to depose Torquay."* Further evidence of the state of the main road to Salcombe lay in the fact that most of the materials needed to build new houses came by boat, as this was the easiest and most economic way to get anything to Salcombe.

Part and parcel of the development of Victorian towns was the influence of the railways. Salcombe was an outpost. The nearest station was more than four miles away but it was not an impossible task to link it to the rail network, and thus the rest of creation, but was it desirable? There were those who saw it as 'the way to go', and there were those comfortably remote in their snug climate living in cosy contentment, well out of the reach of that monster, the Industrial Revolution. Some, with 'feverish pulse', could hardly contain their enthusiasm to import the great iron railroad through their combes into their heartland. The Great Western Railway had set themselves five years to come to terms with the prospect of linking Kingsbridge to Salcombe. It gave people

time to look objectively at the pros and cons, whilst it also gave the railway company time to assess the success of the Kingsbridge branch.

As it turned out the line never got built and Salcombe never did become 'The Princess of Watering Places'; there were those who shouted "Praise the Lord" for that outcome! In 1937 Raymond B. Cattell wrote on this subject, *"Many years ago Salcombe decided by a majority vote that it didn't want the railway. Elsewhere the shop and hotel-keepers by sheer numbers might have defeated such a resolution; for in some places no moral odium attaches to putting bank balances before the beauty and integrity of the homeland. But these were wiser men and their policy of seclusion has justified itself right up to the hilt."* Ironically, had the railways come to Salcombe, they would have long gone by now and left, in their stead, the legacy of a potential cycle path, or a pleasant quiet track, to Kingsbridge through the glorious South Hams countryside away from the busy A381!

Salcombe still continued to grow but in a dignified way. The more discerning (and affluent) types spread the word regarding the delights of this select place and large, grand houses started springing up on the hillsides, all keen to get a glimpse of the estuary. However there were episodes when even this quiet backwater was drawn into conflict on a world-wide scale.

Just before midnight on Sunday, 21 March 1917 the *Asturias*, sailing from Avonmouth to Southampton, was torpedoed by a German submarine, near Salcombe, even though she had every possible light shining on her to display the huge red crosses showing her war-time function. The torpedo lodged in a three ton stack of sulphur and deadly fumes enveloped the hospital ship (previously a Royal Mail liner). In an appalling state, the vessel made it into Salcombe, the decks littered with sixty-eight bodies and other crew members dangerously ill from the poisonous gases. Survivors were taken to the Salcombe Hotel but eight more died there.

The influx of wealthy people to the area continued in the 1920s and in 1928, one gentleman, with an extremely long name, acquired a lovely house called Sharpitor. Otto Christop Jos Gerrard Ludwig Overbeck (Otto for short!), was an inventor who created the first machine for vibro massage. He was a great believer in the use of electricity in dealing with medical problems and experimented on others and himself. He had his successes and his failures. By the age of forty he had gone bald, but by trying all sorts of treatments, when he reached the age of sixty he again had a full head of hair! However his attempts to pass an electric current through a bed on which he was lying, not only had shocking consequences but also burnt him so badly that a spell of eighteen months

in hospital followed.

He was an avid collector of natural history items and was greatly interested in life forms of all shapes and sizes. He believed that the appliance of science could enable people to live until they were 350 years old and was keen to lead by example. However he fell short of this target in 1937 by a mere 265 years! He was a fine man and bequeathed his various possessions and land to groups whom he felt would benefit. He wanted his house to be used as a youth hostel and gave the property to the National Trust on condition that it was used for this purpose. Details of the gardens at Sharpitor are given in my book *The South Hams*.

George Edward Cove was born a son of Salcombe parents. He had the sea in his blood but on a much grander scale than those who simply messed about in boats. In an illustrious career, which spanned half a century, he rose to become Captain of the *Queen Elizabeth*. Even though he went around the world many times, when he finally retired to Liverpool, in 1952, he remembered his roots and called his house 'Sharpitor' after many happy boyhood hours scrambling over the rocks there.

If it wasn't for the National Trust, people would find great areas of coast and countryside debarred to them as regards access. One of the finest, if not the best, stretches of coast in Britain was handed over to them in June 1928. Mr Stenton Covington, on behalf of the National Trust, accepted 600 acres of land from The Earl of Devon at a ceremony at Bolt Head. The land included coastline on both sides of the estuary extending from the vicinity of Gara Rock, up the Salcombe estuary to Millbay, and from the Courtenay Walk (Courtenay is the family name of the Earls of Devon) at Sharpitor through Bolt Head and on to Sewer Mill Cove. At the time the funds did not extend to acquiring all the coast as far as Bolt Tail, that would have to come later! This ended a lot of worry for some locals as they lived in fear of the speculator who saw the chance of making a fast buck as more inviting than preserving an unspoilt coastline. The very thought of a holiday camp high on these cliffs …!

Salcombe settled back to its privileged role of being a paradise for those with the means to enjoy it. However one man was given a bit of a monstrous scare. It was July 1937 when Sidney Field of Salcombe was on the estuary. As he enjoyed his surroundings he suddenly noticed the surface of the water break near him to reveal a large head, oval-shaped with big bulging eyes, protruding a foot or more. In its wake was an eel-like body of more than twenty feet in length. As it swam around it occasionally flicked its large scaly tail out of the water. Sidney was mesmerised by the strange creature and it was a minute or two before he was compelled to get someone else to witness the monster. By the time he had recruited a witness, the creature had gone! Fortunately many people believed him for two good reasons. Firstly, here was a man who had sailed in foreign waters and who was accustomed to sighting unusual, but identifiable, creatures. And secondly, few weeks earlier, at Redlap Cove near Dartmouth, the head gardener of Cyril Maud had seen a similar monster, which defied all attempts by natural historians to discover what it was. Perhaps Salcombe has its own 'Nessie' – what a positive boon to the tourist trade!

There was great excitement one tea time in May 1939 for the passengers aboard the Salcombe–East Portlemouth ferry. Vic Ford, who was at the helm, could hardly believe his eyes either! Swimming, literally just a yard or two away from the small ferry, was a twenty foot long blue-nosed shark. Amidst shrieks of fear, the shark, with its dorsal fin revealing its every menacing movement, swam up and down amongst yachts and other small craft moored nearby. Boatmen hearing the commotion leapt into action. The

*Western Morning News,*which covered the story the next day, finished their account, *"Armed with boat hooks, boatmen gave chase to the intruder, and sporting guns were fetched, but the shark did not stay long enough to be subjected to the bombardment that was being prepared for it."* The shark obviously felt the threat of this was too much to bear so swam towards the safety of the rocks near the estuary mouth.

But excitement like this was the exception rather than the rule and most folk lived quiet, uneventful but very long lives...

Batson had its own 'landmark' until 1935 in the shape of Jacob Terrell. He would sit, on fine days, in the doorway of his cottage and give every passer-by a friendly greeting. The other residents held this man in great esteem so when it was discovered that he was ninety-nine, going on a hundred years old, a fête was held in the village street, to celebrate his 100th birthday. To quote the local paper, "The children danced the Flora past his cottage," as part of the celebrations. He chugged on cheerfully for just one more month before quietly passing away.

Britain's population had soared in Victorian times and with it came a need for more enlightened souls to escape from the more populous and polluted regions to places like Salcombe, ideal for those seeking inspiration when putting pen to paper in those pre-word processing days.

Alfred Tennyson succeeded William Wordsworth as Poet Laureate in 1850, the same year that he got married. It has been said that the majestic, musical language of the *Lotus Eaters* (1832) was inspired by the atmosphere of Salcombe and its environs. By the time he wrote *Crossing the Bar,* allegedly based on a difficult journey into the mouth of the Salcombe Estuary, and over the dreaded bar there, he was an old and ailing man, aware that he would be more likely to be crossing the styx than the bar again! He was aboard Lord Brassey's *Sunbeam* as he entered Salcombe for the umpteenth time in his long and celebrated life. He was created a peer in 1884 and became the first Baron Tennyson, a title he held until his death, at the age of 83, in 1892.

Alfred Austin and Robert Bridges were the next successive holders of the honour of Poet Laureate. John Masefield became the sixteenth and he happily waxed lyrical about this small South Devon port:

"O the salt sea tide of Salcombe,
It wrinkles into wisps of foam
And the church bells ring in Salcombe
To ring past sailors home.
The belfry rocks as the bells ring,
The chimes are as merry as a song,
They ring home wandering sailors
Who have been homeless long."

One of the greatest minds of this century spent a few summers in the sheltered waters of this estuary in the 1930s. The world famous psychologist, Raymond B. Cattell, wrote a book, possibly the best book ever written about this part of Devon, called *Under Sail Through Red Devon.* It was first published in 1937, but is available today under the title *Under Sail Through South Devon and Dartmoor.* He tells of a journey, over sea and land in South Devon and features a few chapters on Salcombe and its estuary. I have included some excerpts here to whet your appetite. He too crossed that same bar at the mouth and wrote the following: *"On either side the little bays and golden sands of Salcombe beckon. Where is there sand of a lovelier, livelier hue than this? Wondrously they beckon to the sea-weary mariner and to add glamour to their call they are sprinkled in*

summer with sprawling sirens in many-coloured bathing costumes.

"Through the limpid pale green waters we can clearly see the yellow sand of the bar, eight feet, six feet, and now four feet beneath our keel. As it shallows we see the rocky islands, marked by lantern poles – the molars which grind the victims caught by the

fangs of the bar. For though we drift languidly now, lulled to the languor by the pleasant sights and sounds, Salcombe can present a very different aspect to the sailor. I have seen the beauty of its other face in winter, when the gale thunders harshly through the dripping, straining pine woods and howls furiously against the black buttresses of Bolt Head. Then the bar is a death-trap for any homing sailor and all too many have come to grief there. It stretches – a white line of raging waters – from the eastern bank to within a stone's throw of the high western cliff, leaving the narrowest of safe passages, and it may well be called the most dangerous bar on the south coast. Even in summer there are many yachtsmen who will not dare to enter after dark, and since the tide may be unsuitable during the day it is something of a feat to get into Salcombe, a feat which so exhausts some that, once accomplished, they drop anchor and go ashore for the rest of the season!"

That Salcombe, which Ray Cattell entered, hasn't changed a great deal since, as this description he penned in the 1930s holds true. "*By some miracle of mercy, Salcombe, in spite of its incomparable natural beauty, has remained one of the few completely unspoilt gems of Devon. Its compact little streets are neat and clean but quaintly old-fashioned, its tasteful villas are in lovely grounds where every kind of tree seems to flourish. If it must spawn characterless terraces it chooses to do so over the hill away from the river.*"

During the last war the Americans commandeered a stretch of coastline in Start Bay (see *The South Hams*) for their preparations for the Normandy landings. Their presence in Salcombe was considerable and has left its mark in a number of ways. However, apart from the occasional plaque and a shop name, there is not a lot of visible reminders of that presence.

And so the years have passed and Salcombe 'The Bride of the Sea' has maintained a low profile with a steady but small amount of growth, enough to be noticeable but not enough to overwhelm. However it was thrown into the limelight in the 1970s when a still unsolved mystery first shrouded the town and district .

The media descended on Salcombe in 1975 when Pat Allen and her two children disappeared without trace. There were no clues as to why she should suddenly have left the town with her two young children without warning. The suspicious nature of the case was enough for the police to make extensive enquiries in a bid to find them and rule out murder. In most cases of this type, some shred of evidence, however thin, usually comes to light but here we have a complete mystery. Why did she leave a wardrobe full of new clothes behind? Why hasn't there been any sighting of this trio? Her passport had expired so there appeared no way that she could have left the country with her children. It is difficult to lead a life without some form of identification or personal documentation but no leads of this type have ever emerged. The police left no stone unturned and contacted every possible organisation and agency but drew a complete blank. The obvious conclusion is that Mrs Allen and her two children were murdered. Helicopters and detection equipment failed to find anything or anyone. Tracker dogs, given scent, got nowhere.

The last sighting of her and her children was at Malborough on carnival day, which she attended with her husband. A gold necklace of hers found its way to a jeweller in the North of England but blood stains found on it were not proved to be that of Pat Allen. *Tales of the Unexplained in Devon* by Judy Chard gives more details of 'Salcombe's Dark Mystery', but unfortunately no more answers.

Throughout the years the rich and the famous have used Salcombe as their playground, the perfect place to recharge their batteries, or simply to get away from the rat race of life. Guests to the Marine Hotel included film stars Jack Hawkins and Peter O'Toole, and writer Paul Gallico. The 1992 Regatta saw a rich vein of talent in the town. Rik Mayall, Gary Glitter, Christopher Timothy, Simon Gregson and Chloe Newsome (Steve McDonald and girlfriend Vicky from *Coronation Street*), Kevin Lloyd, Jane Rossington (*Crossroads*) and the *Neighbours'* twins Gillian and Gayle Blakeney all took time off to be in Salcombe. Indeed there probably were more 'soap' stars in Salcombe than there were on television that week!

Salcombe came close to extended royal patronage in 1812 when Sir Thomas Tyrwhitt, the Gentleman Usher of The Black Rod and also Lord Warden of the Stannaries, was instructed by the Prince Regent (later to be George IV) to find him a suitable place on the south coast where he could spend a great deal of time and where there was sea bathing. Tyrwhitt thought long and hard and knew that Salcombe's climate was the complete opposite of his pet project, the development of the wastelands of Dartmoor at Princetown. He visited Salcombe, staying, appropriately, at the King's Arms. After surveying the district, he came to the conclusion that the best choice would be to construct a bathing pavilion at Splat Cove. Although the plans were considered seriously, over a period of years, the project was abandoned. Had it reached fruition the name 'Regis', reflecting royal patronage, may have been added. However there is already a Salcombe Regis in East Devon, just a mile or so from Sidmouth. Two places with exactly the same name would have caused even more problems than the two Salcombes do now! The major excitement these days is confined to activities that are based on the water, a commodity in great abundance in this neighbourhood, at least at high tide...

When the tide is in, the Salcombe or Kingsbridge Estuary is a wide expanse of water, an impressive sheet so inviting for yachtsmen and so pleasant on the eye. But when the tide is out ... it is a wide expanse of mud that has its own peculiar qualities. Some bright spark once thought that part of the regatta festivities would be enhanced if people could be enticed to race on this oozing morass of a muddy mess. Human nature being what it is, there is never any shortage of volunteers keen to squelch and stagger over this unyielding surface in a bid for a bit of mud and glory! The super-human types endure a quarter mile of mud frolics whilst lesser beings slog through a few hundred yards. The St John Ambulance, those stalwarts of society, stand by just in case someone takes a sharp intake of mud. A fire hydrant on Whitestrand Quay removes the accumulated mud from all the various orifices where it may have secreted itself – the mind boggles!

Occasionally the highest tides at Salcombe, if combined with certain wind conditions, can make life difficult for those who live in the low-lying parts of the town. In October 1939 the following paragraph appeared in the local newspaper: "*Abnormal flooding due to the high southerly wind and spring tides was experienced at Salcombe during the weekend, where houses on the sea front were flooded to a foot deep in their ground floor rooms and furniture was floating around. Fore St was impassable for some time during the evening and people going to the cinema had to be pick-a-backed by an ARP warden who volunteered his services in long waders.*"

The higher parts of Salcombe are immune from floods, the ideal place to live. Most of the roads are laid out in terraces and contour the slopes of the hills. There are many expensive, almost exclusive, houses in Salcombe, some of which have entertained some celebrated guests...

Woodcot is just above Salcombe Castle, a large house with a few stories to tell. The

Dartington-born, celebrated historian, James Antony Froude lived here in the last years of his life. He was a controversial character first at odds with his religious peers and then with other eminent historians who felt a lot of his writings were inaccurate, misinterpreted or both! When he had convinced himself he was right nothing, not even proven fact, would persuade him to change his views. We all know people like that but they do not always endear themselves and Froude had his critics. Perhaps travelling world wide when he was able, and living in Salcombe when he wasn't, steered him clear of more disagreements! But he was famous in his day as he had the common touch, that ability to write in a way which appealed to people.

His writings reflected his life. He went on journeys to Ireland, New Zealand, Australia, the West Indies and South Africa and every journey became a book! However his greatest work was a twelve volume effort titled *A History of England from the fall of Wolsey*. At Salcombe he continued to enjoy as much fresh air as he could. In his prime he had sailed the seas and walked the moors. A contemporary of his described some of his abilities, "No horse could throw him and no storm could make him sea-sick." Here he also found peace and quiet and was buried in the cemetery in 1894.

Several generations ago, at Woodcot, a young girl in the employ of a wealthy couple was accused of theft. Despite protestations of innocence, the finger of blame was firmly pointed in her direction. At 'prayers' that night, when everyone in the large house was assembled, the master and mistress announced that the girl was to be taken into custody the next morning. The next morning she was not to be found. The fact that her belongings were still in her room lead her colleagues to fear the worse. One had even thought they had seen someone scurrying down to Limpyer Rocks. A few weeks later their fears were confirmed when her badly decomposed body was washed up along the coast at Hope Cove. The reaction in Salcombe to the way the theft accusation was handled, and the way the young servant girl was treated, was one of uniform hatred directed at the owners. They were hissed at by many people in the street and were so harassed that they sold up and left Salcombe as soon as they could.

About 1930 there was another drowning, this time probably an accident. Crosbie Garstin was a travel writer of his day and at times was known to pen the odd bit of poetry. One of his poems, *George Peter's Rock* turned out to be sadly prophetic.

"Black is the night with the tide-rips fuming
Over the harbour … songs and laughter
Echo round the old inn rafter…
It's a pale woman I keep tryst with
She slips quietly out of the mist with
Never a sound but the water drips,
And it's cold, cold lips
I'm kissed with.
Her foam-white arms go over and around me,
And her green hair binds me as it bound me
On that first night she rose from the deep,
Lulled me to sleep
And drowned me!"

South Sands, Bolt Head Hotel etc.

Crosbie came to Salcombe and moored his boat. He got dressed up in his glad rags and went ashore to have a good time at a dance. Afterwards he left and, rather than wait for a friend to take him back to his vessel, he decided to swim for it. After all he was a strong swimmer and had swum in much more dangerous waters than the sheltered and relatively safe haven of Salcombe. Alas, in the pitch black of that night he never made it back to his boat, having perished in the attempt to get there.

Long before the days of fibre optics, Salcombe was the scene of the bringing ashore of the English end of the French-Atlantic telegraph cable that linked France with London. The first land fall point was Starehole Bottom, on 28 May 1870, and a house was constructed ready to receive it. After weeks of trying, the communications link was deemed as unsuitable so was removed to nearby North Sands. Here, some eighteen months later, the job was completed to everyone's expectations. The building constructed to house the machinery receiving it is now a cottage – Cable Cottage!

With such a water-orientated community the need for brave persons to be on stand-by to go to the help of those in distress has been evident for several generations.

The first Salcombe lifeboat (1869) was called the *Rescue* and was the generous gift of Richard Durant of Sharpham House, Ashprington. The latter is a conspicuous building on the west bank of the Dart Estuary, a short distance from Totnes and the village pub at Ashprington is called The Durant Arms. Up to the time of writing, there have been eight versions of the Salcombe Lifeboat.

The saddest day in its history was probably 16 October 1916 when the Salcombe lifeboat, *William and Emma* went to the help of the *Western Lass,* a Plymouth schooner, which had gone aground at Lannacombe Bay, a few miles east of Salcombe. The autumnal gales, so much a problem around the coastline of the South West peninsular, had contrived to produce almost impossible conditions. The crossing of Salcombe's notorious bar, in such terrible conditions, was an ordeal for the crew. Unbeknown to them, the crew of the stricken vessel had already been rescued. They sailed on through the storm and eventually reached the *Western Lass*, only to discover that she had been vacated.

There was nothing else that could be done so they turned homewards for Salcombe. Disaster struck near the mouth of the Salcombe Estuary. An enormous wave caught the lifeboat in the stern and threw it high into the air. The men were all thrown into a heap on one side of the boat, tangled with various bits of equipment. Before they could do much about their plight, another monster wave capsized the boat. Only two of the fifteen crew survived, Bill Johnson and Eddie Distin.

The inquest, on 3 November 1916, cited the pros and cons for Salcombe having chosen this particular type of boat several years earlier. The non-righting vessel had been selected because it was more spacious and had better sailing qualities than the self-righting boat. We shall never know how destiny may have treated a different lifeboat! Eddie Distin was a remarkable man and was cox'n for thirty years. Bill Johnson never recovered fully from the ordeal, and died a few years after the disaster.

Salcombe's lifeboat is one of the busiest in Britain and its work spans a wide range of rescue types. It was chosen as the subject of a television documentary series that followed the crew in their work and through their various routines. You can read of their exploits if you wait for the ferry to Portlemouth as details of rescues are recorded there in black and white, literally!

It is hard to imagine Salcombe as a manufacturing centre but, according to experts, in their own field, Salcombe produces the best ice-cream in Britain! Americans, Herb Wolff and Carol Robbins are the writers of the best-selling guide to ice-cream in the USA. They took a 'bus man's holiday' around the world and sampled some three thousand varieties before proclaiming that the best UK ice-cream was that of Salcombe! It certainly takes some licking!

An aerial view of Salcombe

So far we have concentrated our attentions to the west bank of this estuary, but all the while the high and steep slopes opposite have been there looking down on us, awaiting to see what we might say about them...

East Portlemouth is small and follows the West Country pattern of being an east bank settlement smaller than its west bank neighbour. However in the past it was relatively more important than it is today. It was mentioned in the *Domesday Book* and its fine location, with rich and sheltered farmlands and the estuary and sea on the doorstep,

Looking towards Sharpitor and South Sands

supported a population well in excess of Salcombe! It was only in the early part of the nineteenth century when it began to decline as the west bank became the favoured side.

High on that hill is East Portlemouth's church, dedicated to St Winwaloe. This saint is also referred to as Onalaus or Onslow (there is Onslow Road in Salcombe) these being local names for St Winwaloe, a Breton saint who was reputed to never sit down at church services. This, of course, is likely as very few seats were found in churches at that time! The celebrated Rev. Sabine Baring-Gould, a man who loved the architecture of churches, and who travelled widely across the South West gathering folk songs and ballads, was uncomplimentary about the restoration work carried out here, the phrase "barbarously restored" summing up his opinion. The restoration work had been funded by the Dowager Duchess and Duke of Cleveland, owners of the manor.

Buried in the churchyard at Portlemouth is a farmer who was murdered by his apprentice girl. The epitaph, which is now impossible to read as the inscription has been worn away, said:

"Through poison strong he was cut off,
And brought to death at last;
It was by his apprentice girl,
On whom there's sentence past.
O may all people warning take,
For she was burned to a stake."

The date which accompanied this sorry episode was 25 May 1782. The girl was tried in Exeter and, after execution, was cremated.

Close to the belfry door is a large grave that contains the skeletons of six French men, even though seven were recovered, who were aboard the schooner called the *Pauline*, which shipwrecked near the Rickham Coastguard Station, a short distance away. This ship was wrecked on 15 October 1877 and the bodies were picked up by local fishermen.

East Portlemouth, like every other maritime venue in the South West, was a den of smuggling. An unusual consequence of these nefarious activities was the demolition of the village's two pubs. The landowner, The Duke of Cleveland, was so unhappy about the extent of the trade that he ordered them to be pulled down, along with several houses, so that the smugglers would find it impossible to continue. It was also intended as a gesture to deflate and demoralise. Thus the village is unusual in not having a pub today!

The stretch of coastline from Bolt Head to Bolt Tail has long been regarded as a prime graveyard for shipping, with more than forty significant wrecks, on this five mile length of South Devon coast. In simple terms, it is like a huge inhospitable wall that almost seems to attract ships in stormy weather. There is a theory, so far unproved, that ships' compasses are affected by the metal content in these cliffs. This has been suggested by ships' captains running aground in foggy, calm conditions. It is a better excuse than admitting to a lousy piece of navigation ("What 400 foot cliffs?")

The most publicised shipwreck was of the *Herzogin Cecilie*, a windjammer of exquisite beauty and a ship which stole the hearts of all who sailed on her. She was exceptional, a champion of the high seas, eight times winner of the unofficial grain race from Australia.

Built in Bremerhaven in 1902, she was 334 feet long and her mainmast stretched some 200 feet towards the heavens. Her design and her 56,000 square feet of sail enabled her to set record after record. At about 3,250 tons she was the largest ship on Lloyd's register and management there must have been horrified at the news of the shipwreck.

Captain Erikson was well pleased to have travelled from Australia to the Cornish port of Falmouth in 86 days. His wife, Patricia Bourne, a well known authoress at that time, had a premonition that there would be problems in travelling up the English Channel to Ipswich. Her greatest fears were confirmed in late April 1936. The ship went aground near Sewer Mill Cove (known today as Soar Mill Cove) and there was hope that the Finnish barque might be safely refloated. The twenty-two crew were taken off, as was a young lady from Newton Abbot, a friend of the captain's wife. Even the ship's parrot, despite a fair amount of squawking, was brought ashore. The captain stayed as long as he dared but, despite intense salvage operations, the weather conditions and the way in which she had come to rest, mitigated against an early solution to her plight.

The response of the public was amazing and the *Western Morning News* reported that: "*There was a queue of motor cars over a mile long yesterday afternoon near the scene of the wreck on Bolt Head of the barque* Herzogin Cecilie, *such are the immediate results of media publicity. Spectators came from all parts of Devon and Cornwall and even further afield and it was reliably estimated that at the peak of the period there were over 1,000 cars and ten thousand people in the vicinity. During the weekend 50,000 people must have viewed the wreck.*

"*Spacious as are the rock-crowned cliffs, they seemed to be in all places crowded with thrilled onlookers, and every path from all directions was dotted with moving people. Police controlled a difficult situation admirably.*" Thousands of photographs were taken and many came on the market as postcards, today fetching prices more than a thousand times their original face value.

Some went to extraordinary lengths to capture the graceful four-masted vessel on film. The famous newsreel photographer, John Dored, chartered an aeroplane and then discovered the only way to capture the more impressive shots was to fly down the face of the cliff, a manoeuvre which scared him witless – several times! The film shot that day was presented to cinema-goers that night. This was unusual for the 1930s.

After seven weeks the *Herzogin Cecilie* was hauled to Starehole Bay, near Bolt Head. It was felt that salvage operations would more easily be affected in a more sheltered spot. What they didn't bargain for was the cussedness of the weather, that stuff that never does what you want it to – rainy day barbecues, foggy day sightseeing, and calm day kite flying. The same meteorological gremlins were at work in Starehole Bay and, despite the stringent efforts of the salvage men, a south-easterly gale balked their efforts and did grave damage to the stricken ship.

There was no hope for her and she was condemned to stay there. On 19 January 1939 a brief newspaper report stated that: "*Without warning the famous sailing ship the* Herzogin Cecilie, *which has lain in Starehole Bay at the entrance to Salcombe Harbour, since 19 June 1936, capsized and disappeared yesterday. Wreckage is floating up in the harbour and in the channel.*"

Another shipwreck at Sewer Mill Cove, which drew far less attention because the media of 1765 had not advanced past fast horse riders bearing messages, was that of a vessel transporting statues. In a 'monumental' shipwreck, much of its cargo was salvaged and for several days adorned the various rocks surrounding this deep depression on the coastline. Eventually the statues were taken, by road, to Powderham Castle, near the Exe Estuary, home of the Earl of Devon. He was the major landowner in this part of the South Hams.

The cliffs from Bolt Head to Bolt Tail, are awesome in their height and steepness and any ship going aground was in mortal peril on the sea. Mr Popplestone, a Plymothian, who farmed a stretch on top of these massive, towering cliffs, saw a ship washed into them and, as there was no time to summon assistance, bravely made a perilous descent of them. Dangling dangerously he managed to save the lives of many men. For this action he became the first person to win the Victorian medal, awarded for gallant deeds of this nature.

Two large sea rocks near Sewer Mill are called 'Pixy Dance' on account of the considerable number of pixies who dwell here. It is a reminder that not all these mischievous characters live on or around Dartmoor but, not having seen the maritime equivalent, I cannot vouch for their sartorial elegance. Whether they wear green and red, like their moorland counterparts, remains a mystery only the sailors drowned in the waters off these cliffs are purported to know...

Any book about this area should include the neighbouring hill-top village of Malborough, for it once had Salcombe within its parish; buried in its graveyard are many unfortunate victims of shipwrecks between Bolt Head and Bolt Tail.

Typical is one about twenty yards from the south-west corner of the church, to the Chambers family. The inscription on the slate headstone says, "Here lie the bodies of Rhodes, Daniel, Mary and Joseph Chambers, of Jamaica, who were shipwrecked at Cathole, within this parish. August 23rd, 1757."

The Church of All Saints at Malborough is one of the most distinct and obvious landmarks in the South Hams. The size of the church and the smallness of the congregation posed problems in 1939. The Rev. H. S. Arrowsmith was not a happy man. Members of the congregation had moaned long and loudly that they found it difficult to hear what was being preached. The vicar's response was that the church was ten times too big, which meant that preachers with bad throats or weak voices stood little chance at putting over their evangelical thoughts. In addition, the exposed location of the church meant that on windy days the noise outside was so great that nobody could hear, however voluminous the priest! Arrowsmith's remedy was simple, "The congregation of about fifty on a Sunday evening, scattered over a building capable of seating 500, is more like a collection of isolated individuals who don't want to have anything to do with each other. You should all sit together so nobody has to shout!"

The belfry of this church contains an impressive collection of certificates won by the bellringers. This 'Cathedral of the South Hams' is well worth a visit if you are passing.

Malborough was just one of many places in this area associated with the production of a concoction called 'White Ale', a drink best left to those who worried not about their stomach linings! One of the village pubs brewed this awful ale and its content has long been the source of much debate. It is the 'white' in its name which has produced all sorts of theories as to what this may have been. Some, allegedly in the know, reckoned that the 'grout' was really pigeon's dung and may well have explained away the appearance and the taste of it. The last Malborough manufacturer of this foul brew failed, fortunately, to pass on the secret of its contents but it is known that he kept a lot of pigeons! Another historic source contains the phrase, "tastes as if pigs had wrestled in it!" Sir Garrard Tyrwhitt-Drake, of Maidstone in Kent, claimed in 1900 that it was made

in his home county and there was no hint of pigeon's droppings in their brew.

The South Hams reveals more of the secrets and 'delights' of White Ale! You will also be able to read the tale of a Malborough man who, on his death bed, predicted trouble if he was not, "buried before Midday!"

For several years we have produced walking books, some have included gargantuan strolls, which only the superfit or the supermad have been able to do. However our most popular walks have proved to be those which are less than five miles and which do not

demand all the equipment one would normally carry on a trek to the Poles! Here are three little strolls in this patch. There is no magic wand we can wave to remove the hills, cliffs or steep slopes so we suggest you take your time, choose the right day and pace yourselves on the tougher slopes. Remember that if you do these walks in the height of the summer season, then parking may be a problem – crisp Spring mornings are ideal but we can't always be that choosy!

South Sands is aptly named because it is the last beach of any note on the west side of the estuary before the open sea. There is a small paying car park at The Tides Reach opposite and behind the original lifeboat station, built in 1877 and used until about 1925. However if you are based in Salcombe town it is a pleasant ferry ride to South Sands and removes the need to park. As a possible incentive to those reluctant to walk, several hotels offer cream teas, in the season, and you can always treat yourself at the end of this fantastic walk. Walking out to Bolt Head, having eaten one, is ill-advised. Stout shoes are suggested for this circular stroll of about 3 miles as there are many places where exposed rocks make underfoot conditions painful for those with thin soles.

From the old lifeboat station climb the steep hill behind it. It is a no through road that leads to Sharpitor and some other fine properties. The first burst is along the road but will enable you to get into your stride, but as it is just a leisurely stroll, of a few hours, there is no need to rush. Soon a gate is reached to Overbecks. Pass through it and head up the drive. After a hundred yards or so there is a forking of the routes. Take the left one which is marked 'Bolt Head Via Stare Hole Bay.' If you are feeling suitably benevolent, make a donation to The National Trust at this point. A reduction in your small change will mean less weight to carry up the cliffs!

Views of the sea will be limited along the first section because of the trees that line this pedestrian only thoroughfare (winter walkers fare slightly better). The way ahead is uncomplicated and soon the trees thin out and disappear giving views south-eastwards along the coast to Prawle Point.

As the views open up the path, known, but not signed, as the Courtenay Walk, gets stonier underfoot and rockier by the minute as it passes through fine surroundings.

As a comfort for those who suffer from vertigo, and also as a practical safety measure, the walker's needs are well catered for here. Stone steps are cut in the rock and a hand rail, on the seaward side, prevents anyone from slipping over the edge in the most potentially precarious stretch of the path.

The path passes beneath Sharp Tor's many grand rockpiles and turns to enter Stare

Hole Bay from a lofty access point. Continue onwards and in a short distance a sort of hanging valley reaches the coast a short way ahead. This is Starehole Bottom, and if you turn your back to the sea and look up it bears a striking resemblance to Dartmoor. However the rock type is very different – instead of granite it is a metamorphic schist!

A signpost offers a choice of routes but as Bolt Head is so near it would be foolish not to make the extra bit of effort needed to scale its dizzy heights. If you need an excuse to pause to catch your breath, the view is worth looking at. Examine, from here, the path you have just come along and you will appreciate why those railings were put in further back on the Courtenay Walk!

A granite seat provides a resting place for those in need on the high shoulder of this headland and gazes down to two sea bird inhabited rocks – Mew Stone and Little Mew Stone. There are scores of rocks called 'Mew' because it is a local name for a seagull. It is believed this derives from its noise or mewing sound.

A short distance ahead with two flights of eight steps is the now redundant coast-guard look-out. From here a wide expanse of sea can be surveyed, and down channel the Eddystone Lighthouse is visible in the right conditions.

The next point to head for can be seen about 300 yards away in the shape of a signpost on top the cliff. As you approach it the slope becomes far steeper and the sign temporarily disappears from view.

When you reach it you will probably be impressed at the extent of what you can see if you are familiar with the Devonshire topography. Apart from a large proportion of the South Hams, it is possible to identify many of southern and eastern Dartmoor's hills. From the west Shell Top, Three Barrows, high above the Erme valley, and Rippon Tor can be spied. Observant folk will just be able to pick out the top of Haytor Rocks, 25 miles away as the crow (or is it seagull?) flies!

Do not cross the stile, unless of course you want to go on a much longer and tougher safari. Turn right along the route which is marked 'Malborough – South Sands – Overbecks'. This path starts off as a level, grassy corridor running beside a wall. After a few hundred yards it starts to dip gently and then more steeply. On such sections you begin to question whether it is better to go downhill rather than up! Ignore any routes that bisect your line, descend down into Starehole Bottom and cross its stream for the second time today. A stepped slope leads up and out of this valley.

Towards the top of this slope you will hear a gurgling stream. A choice of routes presents itself again. A bit of self discipline will see you continue on to 'Sharp Tor – Overbecks'. With the fence on your left, and the steep gully of Starehole Bottom on your right, you will easily reach the top of Sharp Tor. Here is the best view in the district of the Salcombe River. The bollard or capstan is a memorial to W. Newton Drew of Ringrone, a large house we shall pass later near Overbecks. It is a most informative oracle with a compass and sight lines indicating the direction and distances of familiar places and landmarks, ideal if your sense of direction is awry.

When you have had your fill of the view, continue on in the general direction of

Salcombe, a kingdom of grand houses it appears from here!

After a short time, one of those redundant trig. points appears on the left. From here Malborough's church tower forms a distinct landmark. Beyond, and in the distance, it is possible to fathom the outline of the china clay workings of Lee Moor on the western fringe of the moor.

The path drops down and the scrubby vegetation obscures the view of the estuary and Salcombe. At the bottom of a flight of steps a T-junction is encountered. Turn right and go downhill. The path now twists and turns this way and that before reaching Overbecks. The vegetation with its exotic tropical appearance is striking as the entrance to the property is soon reached. From here the way back to South Sands is all downhill, through a wooded environment punctuated by large houses. Stay on the zig-zagging surfaced road and float back to the start and possibly a cream tea in style!

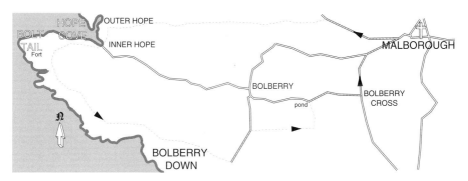

Malborough, on the roof of the South Hams, is the starting place for this second circular stroll, this time of about six miles. The nature of the narrow streets can cause traffic problems, particularly in summer, so you may need to hunt around for a suitable parking spot. The walk begins from the exit to the church at the spire end and, as this is the most obvious landmark in the South Hams, should be easy to find.

The signpost says that this meeting of four roads is called Malborough Green. A cottage called 'Four Ways' stands between two ways, one to the left to Bolberry and Soar, the other to the right and Hope Cove. Our way lies initially along that road but don't despair as this road walking section at the start only amounts to a few minutes. It has its compensations for the walker sees more than the motorist, specially in a land of high hedgerows. A good example is on a thatched cottage on the right at the very start of the walk. A little sun with a number beneath it probably is an insurance plaque. At one time, if you were insured the fire tender came, but if not you were at the mercy of the elements and any help that could be mustered at short notice.

Continue along this road past the raised reservoir and the turning right to Withymore Farm and its Rugwell Herd.

A short distance farther along is a footpath signposted to the left, marked by a stone near the bottom of the hedge. Leave the road and head for the gateway about 50 yards across the field. An orange arrow suggests the general direction to go, which is across the ridge of the field to the next gateway. For those of you who have started looking at the views, it will now be apparent that this is a landscape of wide views and, provided the prevailing westerly wind is not too keen, those views will be enjoyed.

At the next gateway the way ahead is not obvious so walk down the field keeping the

right hand hedge parallel. A gap in the hedge, which looms up ahead, by a small tree has been used by those who have passed this way before to reach the next field. Follow the left hedge and it will lead you to a gateway that can be exceedingly soft. The red Devon soil can be a squidgy substance and many a good pair of trousers has been given a red tide-mark in gateways like this one!

For the next three quarters of a mile or so, all that is really necessary in navigating skills is to keep the hedge to your left; in theory nothing can go wrong…

To your right, down in the dip, is the sprawling hamlet of Galmpton, its church looking neat like something out of a model village.

We are heading seawards with the sweep of Bigbury Bay filling the forward view. Keep going through all gateways, remembering to close them afterwards. Don't worry about the lack of arrows, you will soon start to drop down to Hope Cove. The latter has shown a growth in bungalows in recent years and eventually we drop down beside them passing along a lane that skirts their back gardens.

Walk downhill and the church of St Clements, complete with bell, will be reached straight ahead at a junction. A flight of steps descends on the left side of St Clements, and we go down them to meet a signpost. If you want to take time out to explore Outer Hope to the right, or Inner Hope to your left, then that is your prerogative. There are several places where you can wine and dine.

Hope Cove is a picturesque place, represented at the Royal Academy, in London, by two paintings by the maritime artist, Hook, who painted 'Crabbers' and 'Seaside Ducks' here.

Our way lies to the left and down the hill towards the old lifeboat station. Here a signpost shows the way up to Bolt Tail, our next destination. Now we are on the coastal footpath and it is a conveyor belt of walkers, a never-ending supply of fresh-air freaks who delight in walking the cliffs but are rarely spotted in the lanes and on the public rights of way away from the coast. Carry out your own survey if you don't believe me!

It is a bit of a climb up to Bolt Tail's promontory fort but worth the effort. There are many pathways, but if you climb to the highest point you will not get lost. The view down the channel takes in the Eddystone Lighthouse, Rame Head and beyond. It is also possible to pick out such landmarks as Burgh Island closer to home.

The next stretch is spectacular and takes you along the coast in the direction of Salcombe. However we are only staying on top these precipitous cliffs for about a mile to Bolberry Down. Unfortunately the general trend is upwards but a north-westerly wind could provide a helping push from the rear!

Bolberry Down is conspicuous by its three tall masts so, again, there is no excuse to miss it!

The surface underfoot is conducive for walking and there is much to delight the eye. If you have wayward children with you, it would be worth keeping them well away from the cliff edge, particularly if it's at all windy.

At the top of the cliff is a stile. After you have dragged your weary bones over it, turn left and follow the wall inland staying on the level to make a bee-line for the masts ahead. After several hundred yards, the flat roofed Port Light Hotel and Restaurant is reached. Just head to the right, the masts of Bolberry, so long in view, are reached.

Take the road on the left that passes all three masts. A few hundred yards on the right is a footpath named Jacob's Lane. Turn right and follow this thoroughfare to its end. This is a bridleway and you don't have to be Tonto to work out that horse riders use this lane! The first eastward section is level with a few wet spots but after several hundred yards it veers sharply left and drops downwards to join a road by a mucky looking pond. A seat here enables weary wayfarers to enjoy the aquatic splendour!

Turn right and trek up the road to Bolberry Cross and if you see a fine lady on a white horse … tell her she's in the wrong county! Turn left and walk back along the road to Malborough, whose church will now be a welcome sight, whatever your denomination!

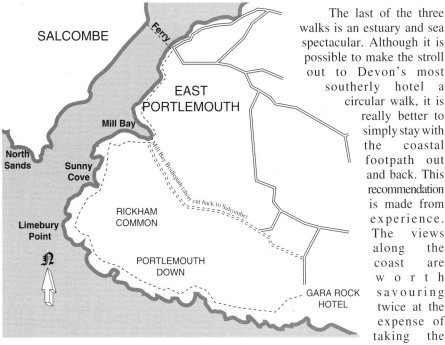

The last of the three walks is an estuary and sea spectacular. Although it is possible to make the stroll out to Devon's most southerly hotel a circular walk, it is really better to simply stay with the coastal footpath out and back. This recommendation is made from experience. The views along the coast are worth savouring twice at the expense of taking the customary alternative cut inland, the Mill Bay Bridle path, and down the small valley that runs back to Mill Bay.

If Salcombe is the starting point, it will be necessary to cross the ferry to the East Portlemouth side. The ferry crossing is about an eighth of a mile. If you calculated how much 'pro rata' it would cost to sail to the USA on this ferry, you would discover that the fare would be wildly more expensive than the most luxurious cruise ship! Perhaps it's a bad analogy for it is unlikely that the opportunity will arise. The argument for the apparently expensive tariff is that the alternative way of travelling between Salcombe and East Portlemouth is a road journey of more than twenty miles on roads where a gallon of petrol will not take you very far at a speed barely faster than that experienced in the days of the stage coach. The last ferryman to row his customers across was Ferryman Distin, who developed very broad shoulders as his services were in great demand. A motor ferry service was introduced in 1911.

Once across the 'other' side you will soon forget the economics of all this as the scenery and the relaxed atmosphere will soon take over. Stroll southwards along the road with its many 'private' signs and privacy-seeking fences. You may catch a glimpse of Small's Cove, which is small! Small's House caught fire in 1911 and the Salcombe fire brigade had to take their horse drawn fire engine to it on the ferry!

Many years ago it was common to see the beach covered with crab pots. At the turn of the century, when fishermen's wives were busy on the beach, they would often sit their children inside the crab-pots as they made excellent, restraining playpens.

With that graphic thought in your mind, continue until you reach Mill Bay. Here you will see the remains of a concrete slipway. This was built in the last war by the United States Naval Constructional Battalion. At this point they repaired landing craft that had been damaged in the D-Day landings. It is a fact that many would-be walkers have intended to do the walk set out here only to get as far as the golden sands of Mill Bay and go no further. But you are not allowed to mutiny! Continue on taking the closest footpath, right, to the water, not the higher cliff path. Your chosen route is one that rises and falls, with regularity, for the next mile or so.

After the aptly named Sunny Cove is passed, there are tremendous views across the mouth of the estuary to the twin inlets of South Sands and North Sands. This bit of the South Devon Coastal Footpath is one of the most popular with walkers but, being close to Salcombe (and by that token, civilisation), many of the people you will pass are 'casual' walkers and will be evident by their choice of footwear, ranging from sensible trainers down to open sandals, hardly ideal for this type of terrain! The way ahead is along the winding lower coast path and Bolt Head's towering cliffs become more obvious as Rickham Common, or at least the edge of it, is traversed. Here there used to be a nine hole golf course at one time. This is one amenity lacking in this district, even though there have been several attempts to establish one.

The general trend of the coastal path is upwards. It passes through great outrops of that type of rock which is classified as a metamorphic schist, which forms a broad band across the southern tip of South Devon. Our destination is Gara Rock, which eventually comes into sight only when we are close to it. It is reached after a bit of toil but hopefully no trouble as long as we don't try to climb up any of the rockpiles along the way!

The hotel is the ideal location to get refreshments before returning to Salcombe. It has an interesting history, having started out in life as the Rickham Coastguard Station in the 1840s. In 1909 it became a guest house, and over the years has evolved into a fine hotel.

Through the years many famous people have stayed here, an ever-growing list includes Sir Laurence Olivier, Margaret Rutherford and Sir John Betjeman, making yet another Poet Laureate in the neighbourhood to enjoy the poetic views!

Many films or television programmes have been shot in this vicinity and, for more details, you should read my book *Made In Devon,* which covers the whole county and which makes fascinating reading. Betty St John and Michael Craig filmed scenes for *High Tide at Noon* in 1957. This was a film about fishermen in Nova Scotia – how deceitful the film makers can be!

Nigel Havers came to Gara Rock whilst filming the BBC production of R. F. Delderfield's *A Horseman Riding By.*

Refreshed and relaxed, the romp back to Salcombe can begin. There is a choice. Those who want a short cut and save themselves a mile, should walk down the drive of the Gara Rock Hotel. A short distance on, just past the first bend, will find a footpath signed to the left. On the horizon you will see Malborough Church ahead. Cross the fields and follow the way down into the narrow valley that leads gently down to Millbay. However, if the energy reserves permit, it is far better to return along the coast path. The views always look different the other way and, as you enter the Salcombe Estuary, you will once more begin to see why so many people fall in love with this most southern of Devonshire places!

OTHER OBELISK PUBLICATIONS THAT FEATURE THIS AREA:

The South Hams, Chips Barber	48pp	£2.50
Burgh Island & Bigbury Bay, Chips Barber & Judy Chard	32pp	£2.50
Walks in the South Hams, Brian Carter	32pp	£1.95
Under Sail Thr South Devon & Dartmoor, R. B. Cattell	160pp	£2.99
Tales of the Unexplained in Devon, Judy Chard	48pp	£2.50
Made in Devon, Chips Barber and David FitzGerald	104pp	£2.99

Around & About Salcombe